T0380283

THE SECRETS OF
A CHILD LEFT BEHIND

Hope was not lost...

MISS VEGAS

authorHOUSE®

AuthorHouse™
1663 Liberty Drive
Bloomington, IN 47403
www.authorhouse.com
Phone: 833-262-8899

Published by AuthorHouse 02/15/2024

ISBN: 979-8-8230-2249-1 (sc)
ISBN: 979-8-8230-2250-7 (hc)
ISBN: 979-8-8230-2248-4 (e)

Library of Congress Control Number: 2024903679

Print information available on the last page.

Any people depicted in stock imagery provided by Getty Images are models, and such images are being used for illustrative purposes only. Certain stock imagery © Getty Images.

This book is printed on acid-free paper.

CONTENTS

DEDICATION

In profound acknowledgment and heartfelt gratitude, I dedicate this work to the intricate tapestry of my life, woven with threads of both adversity and resilience.

This dedication is a heartfelt tribute to the transformative power of adversity. To my late brother, a formidable warrior who faced cancer with unwavering strength and courage. Though you are no longer by my side, your spirit continues to inspire my every step as your courage became my guiding light.

I extend my deepest appreciation to every individual who played a pivotal role in molding the person I am today. To those who contributed to my upbringing, imparting wisdom and support, you are the architects of my foundation, and your influence resonates in every aspect of my life. Each lesson learned, every challenge faced, and triumph celebrated were woven into the fabric of this dedication.

I extend my appreciation to my supervisors, who showed remarkable understanding during times of domestic violence and provided a sanctuary of empathy and support. I am grateful for your compassion and consideration, which I now carry forward. In the face of personal turmoil, your understanding became a beacon of hope.

To my cherished church circle, whose unwavering encouragement and tireless prayers sustained me through the darkest hours, your faith and camaraderie fueled my strength to endure. With the many prayers, I was able to weather the storms that raged in my life and those collective prayers became a powerful force that lifted me beyond that adversity.

In the loving memory of my daughter, who succumbed to the insidious grip of fentanyl intoxication, your brief yet impactful presence inspires a commitment to fostering understanding among young women and emphasizing the importance of attentive listening, free from judgment or condemnation.

This dedication stands as a testament to the intricate dance of pain and growth. I can say that resilience was born from that pain and now the strength that forged through adversity, and enduring gratitude for those who illuminated my path with compassion, wisdom, and unwavering support.

FOREWORD

In the pages that follow, you are about to embark on a journey that encapsulates the essence of resilience, the strength born from the crucible of unimaginable trials. "Secrets of a Child Left Behind, Hope was not Lost" is a profound narrative that transcends the boundaries of sorrow, weaving a tale of endurance, courage, and the indomitable spirit that refuses to surrender to despair.

This poignant account unveils the tumultuous odyssey of a young girl and her brother, thrust into a world of shadows and hardship after losing their mother to a violent tragedy. Yet, within the depths of darkness, this story seeks not to dwell on despair but to illuminate the flickering ember of hope that persists against all odds.

As the author courageously unravels the complexities of their journey, you will witness the stark realities of a harsh environment, scarred by violence, loss and communal strife. The narrative is an inflicting exploration of the human spirit, navigating treacherous terrain with the unwavering belief that hope, even in its most fragile form, can be a powerful catalyst for transformation.

This is a story of overcoming, not just survival, and it pays tribute to the remarkable strength found in unexpected places. Through tribulations that test the very fabric of existence, the author beckons though tenuous, is clinging to tenaciously.

"Secrets of a Child Left Behind" is a homage to the endurance of the human spirit and a testament to the redemptive power of hope. Prepare to be moved, inspired, and reminded that, even in the darkest hours, the glimmer of hope can be the beacon that guides us back to the light.

PREFACE

In the following pages, the narrative of "Secrets of a Child Left Behind: Hope Was Not Lost" unfolds, revealing a poignant journey marked by resilience, courage, and the enduring strength of the human spirit. This book invites you into a world shaped by both the shadows of tragedy and the illuminating light of hope—a journey that defies despair and underscores the belief that, even in the darkest corners, hope remains steadfast.

This story is a tapestry woven with threads of loss, trauma, and the yearning for love and acceptance. It delves into the complexities of family dynamics, societal challenges, and the personal struggles that mold our identities. Through the eyes of the protagonist, you'll witness the harsh realities of growing up amidst adversity, the impact of absent parental figures, and the echoes of trauma that linger far beyond childhood.

As you embark on this narrative, it is my sincere hope that the experiences shared within these pages serve as more than a chronicle of one individual's life. May it become a source of connection, understanding, and inspiration for those who have faced their own trials, for those seeking hope in the midst of adversity, and for anyone with a heart open to the transformative power of resilience.

This story is a testament to the belief that, even when hope seems distant, it can be found, nurtured, and ultimately become a guiding force towards a brighter tomorrow. Through the journey of "Secrets of a Child Left Behind," we explore the enduring power of hope, the strength it provides in times of darkness, and the transformative impact it can have on the human spirit.

INTRODUCTION

In the haunting shadows of tragedy and the desolate landscape of a forsaken Las Vegas neighborhood, the harrowing tale of "Secrets of a Child Left Behind' unfolds. This poignant narrative follows the lives of a vulnerable four-year-old girl and her three-year old brother, thrust into the abyss of despair after losing their mother to a brutal homicide. Weeks of anguished searching culminate in the heart-wrenching discovery of their mother's lifeless body in the unforgiving desert.

Left in the care of their maternal grandmother, residing in an undeveloped neighborhood of Las Vegas, the children face a harsh reality marked by fear, trauma, and disorientation. The backdrop of their new environment is one of violence, molestation, rape, gang conflicts, and a community grappling with shared challenges but tearing itself apart. In the face of relentless adversity, this book project faced attempts to be aborted, as the forces of darkness sought to silence a story that needed to be told.

Yet against all odds, the author, clinging to a steadfast faith, clung to the belief that God would guide this story to light. "Secrets of a Child Left Behind" is a testament to resilience, a journey through the darkest corridors of human experience, and a testament to the enduring strength of a spirit that refuses to be extinguished.

Chapter One
A Night to Remember

At the tender age of 23, my mother's life met a tragic end, a victim of brutal violence left abandoned in the unforgiving desert. The haunting echoes of that fateful night in 1982 continue to reverberate vividly within my mind, casting a long shadow over the sudden upheaval of my world and that of my little brother.

In the confined living room of my cousin's apartment, where my mother, brother, and I shared a pull-out bed, the unfolding year ushered in a sequence of devastating events. A knock on the front door roused me from sleep, prompting me to alert my mother to the visitor. She rose silently, leaving the door slightly ajar upon her departure. With my brother asleep beside me, I peered through the crack into the darkness of the night, catching indistinct voices on the other side. Little did we know, we stood on the brink of an unforgettable night.

Upon my mother's return, closing the door behind her, an unexpected guest lingered on the other side. As she prepared herself in the bathroom, I followed, perching on the toilet seat. In the ordinary act of applying makeup, she instructed me to lock the door after she left. However, what seemed like a routine night took a foreboding turn as my confident mom, assured of her return, left us behind. Dutifully locking the door, I woke my brother, whispering, "Momma is gone," but he remained in blissful slumber.

The morning brought confusion when my cousin questioned our mother's whereabouts. A fruitless search ensued, and after four days, we found ourselves at my maternal grandmother's— our mom hadn't returned for us. The void left by both parents plunged my brother and me into a disorienting state of fear and abandonment. What began as an ordinary night transformed into a nightmarish reality of horror and emptiness.

The agonizing quest for answers culminated in a police officer arriving at my grandmother's, holding a picture that had to be my mom's. Although unseen, my grandmother confirmed her identity, leaving me torn between relief and anxiety regarding her fate. The revelation of my mom's death unraveled a reality I grappled to comprehend.

Nights became a canvas for unsettling dreams, and on one such night, I dreamt my mom was incarcerated, jolting me awake in terror. The truth, confirmed by my maternal grandmother, was heart-wrenching—my mom was gone. The ensuing days blurred into a tapestry of sorrow, with mourners gathering at my grandmother's house. As the gravity of the situation sunk in, I wandered around proclaiming, "My momma is dead," attempting to reconcile with the irreparable loss.

Funeral day arrived, and we found ourselves in a church, my mother's form concealed within a closed casket, prepared for her final resting place. Beside my brother and me, our silent father had just lost his only wife. The sealed casket shielded the brutal reality—she had been handcuffed, savagely beaten, and abandoned in the desert, where wild dogs mercilessly ravaged her remains.

Post-funeral, we relocated to live with our maternal grandmother. Despite my earnest desire to be with my father, circumstances dictated that my great-grandfather persuaded him to let our grandmother care for us. Legal proceedings held us in limbo, anticipating our father's return, yet he never appeared. The additional layer of abandonment compounded our already shattered world.

Residing in my grandmother's house, alongside her four other children, provided a modicum of solace. Despite the tragic circumstances, we found comfort in the care extended by someone willing to take us in. It wasn't our parents, but given the circumstances, it would have to suffice.

As life settled into a new rhythm, my grandmother and aunt accompanied us to clear out my mom's apartment. Amidst the emotional task, I clung to a poignant memory—the closet held my mom's shoes. With childlike joy, I would slip them on, even though they were too big, cherishing this small connection to my mother amid overwhelming loss.

Chapter Two

Unraveling the Cycle

Ever heard the adage, "Momma's babies, daddy's maybe"? I, for one, yearned for the affection of my mother, firmly believing that every child craves a mother's love for a sense of completeness. In today's society, the well-being of our children hinges on the presence of a healthy home environment. Unfortunately, the harsh reality is that many single mothers find themselves in fatherless homes, shouldering the sole responsibility of raising their children. This trend spans generations, transcending cultural and ethnic backgrounds. As the biblical passage wisely states, "There is nothing new under the sun," and indeed, this phenomenon persists, leaving countless children in unstable homes with undisciplined routines.

In my early journey as a mother, I found myself making choices that weren't particularly healthy for either me or my children. At that time, the concept of distinguishing between healthy and unhealthy decisions wasn't even on my radar. The potential impact on our lives remained veiled, and it took the passage of time for me to realize that my situation wasn't unique. Many others faced similar challenges, sharing my background and circumstances, regardless of their diverse appearances.

Interacting with other mothers and fathers, I discovered a common thread of unhealthy decision-making, especially concerning their children. It felt like a collective struggle, as if we were all navigating an unfamiliar terrain, oblivious to the consequences, exacerbated by the trend of having children at increasingly younger ages. Unveiling the prevalence of these challenges, I learned that many parents, like me, were inadvertently making unhealthy decisions for their children.

I firmly believe that poor decision-making often stems from the values we develop for ourselves along our journey. When we forfeit our identity or the robust values instilled by our parents with positive principles, or when we compromise our integrity, it paves the way for a potentially disastrous life. This rings particularly true in my own narrative; I initiated intimate relationships at a young age, seeking affirmation from the wrong individuals and forsaking the essence of who I truly was and the values instilled in me. I fell in with an older circle of women already immersed in risky behaviors, including substance abuse. Succumbing to worldly temptations, I abandoned my education, becoming entangled in a cycle of drugs that ultimately led to experiences of domestic violence and teenage pregnancy.

Tragedy, I realized, does not discriminate based on social class; it can affect low-income, middle-class, and affluent families alike. Even households with well-educated individuals who believe they have everything under control may find themselves entangled in issues like drug abuse, violence, teenage pregnancies, or parents abandoning their responsibilities. I've observed instances where fathers neglect their roles as protectors, instead demeaning women with derogatory language. Sadly, women, in turn, seem to have lost their virtue, humility, love faithfulness, and self-respect, influenced by a cycle of traumatic and broken relationships that leave them feeling empty and worthless.

This assertion remains impartial; it doesn't solely pertain to lower-income households or families grappling with poverty. It extends its reach to those who have enrolled their children in prestigious schools, to families blessed with abundant financial resources capable of providing their children with every necessity or desire. It encompasses even those families who embrace a lavish lifestyle, driving luxurious cars and residing in mansions atop hills. These parents, too, have come to realize that, despite the extensive material gifts bestowed upon their children, flaws persist. Some find themselves entangled in the grip of drugs or even resort to prostitution, striving to maintain the illusion of societal opulence. To those seeking understanding, it becomes evident that genesis lies within, for the battleground is the arena of our minds.

Reflecting on the formative years of my life, I realized that the primary challenge wasn't rooted in teenage relationships, or the parental values instilled by my grandmother during my early years. Instead, it was the unresolved trauma that cast a shadow over my choices. I found myself navigating through a maze of poor decisions in relationships, mirroring the abusive patterns set by my parents. Insecurity became my companion, leading me to settle for less than I deserve, oblivious to the profound truth that I was wonderfully and perfectly made in Christ.

I've observed that many young women grapple with self-discovery, unsure of their desires and needs. Society has propagated misleading ideals, suggesting that settling for unfaithful partners is acceptable if they provide for us, deeming it the norm. It's crucial for us to return to the righteousness and purity inherent in life and family. A scripture comes to mind, urging us to adopt the mindset of Christ Jesus, emphasizing the battleground of the mind that plagues many. Our collective tolerance for evading accountability has permeated our lives, allowing us to excuse or avoid the truth rather than confront it directly, hindering progress for all humanity. This pattern of dishonesty and the absence of accountability has woven a cycle of negativity and poor values for both us and our children.

I can recall the tumultuous moments between my parents, engaged in physical altercations over reasons unbeknownst to me. What I can attest to is the inception of a recurring cycle that ultimately led to my mother's untimely demise, leaving her two children grappling with the aftermath. The pattern was unmistakable: clashes between my father and mother, her subsequent departure, only to return. One vivid instance etched in my memory involves a heated confrontation, with my father hurling derogatory remarks at her. Oblivious to my presence, he unleashed a torrent of words, sowing seeds of discord in the air. He seemed indifferent to the impact on me as I stood there, absorbing every uttered syllable. The relentless drama took its toll on my mother until she reached a breaking point. Packed with resolve, she gathered our belongings and unequivocally declared her departure, signaling the end of her tolerance for the chaos. Opting to exchange one tumultuous relationship for another, she encountered a man named Moon Dog shortly after severing ties with my father. Despite the unconventional name, she decided to venture into this new chapter, leaving behind the tumult of our familial past for Moon Dog's apartment.

There's a haunting memory etched in my mind when Moon Dog, for reasons lost on me, decided to handcuff my brother and me to the dresser one day. The alleged misdeed that led to this extreme punishment escapes my recollection, and even if we erred, it felt disproportionate to be restrained in such a manner. The experience left me frightened, overwhelmed with a sense of isolation and helplessness. Picture standing in discomfort, bound by metal, with your mother—the pillar of strength, love, and protection—merely observing from the doorway. Can you fathom the fear that permeates when someone is harming you, and your plea for intervention falls on silent ears? I grappled with confusion, desperately hoping for my mother to assert herself, to demand our release from the unforgiving cuffs. Yet, she remained silent, not uttering a single word. Moon Dog, reveling in his perceived dominance, made it abundantly clear that she was powerless to aid us, coldly stating, "Why are you looking at her? She can't help you." Imagine the profound bewilderment, realizing that even your own mother couldn't shield you from harm. I'm grateful to a higher power that, in the midst of this ordeal, we were spared from anything more sinister than the restraints. From where I stood, it seemed there was no protection to be found.

Life has been my most impactful instructor, especially now that I find myself a mother to four vibrant and healthy children. I made a solemn commitment to tirelessly advocate for my children, vowing to shield them from any situation that might leave them feeling powerless. Understanding early on that our surroundings shape who we become, I firmly believe that as parents, we serve as the primary protectors for our children. If we cannot ensure their safety, then who else will?

I aspire that, upon delving into the pages of my book, a narrative rooted in my own experiences, you will undergo a transformative shift in your mindset. My wish is for you to find renewed strength and resilience, persisting in the face of numerous challenges. May you be inspired to make wholesome choices not only for yourself but also for the well-being of your children, recognizing their dependence on you. I hope that this journey prompts you to embrace a life characterized by purpose and fulfillment, regardless of the external circumstances. Remember, in the eyes of God, we are inherently special and accepted just as we are. There's no need for pretense or uncertainty; He embraces you for your authentic self.

For all the mothers and fathers experiencing unhealthy relationships, I want to encourage you to make a change for the lives of your innocent children. Not only do I want you to do it for your children, but I also want you to do it for yourself. I want you to be able to walk in the newness of life, the abundant blessings ready for you to take hold of. If we can't protect our children from hurt, harm, and danger, then who can?

CHAPTER THREE
NAVIGATING SHADOWS

As parents, we often underestimate the profound impact our decisions can have on our children. Whether assuming they are too young to grasp the complexities of the world or believing that they won't remember as they grow older, we sometimes overlook the lasting influence our actions can wield. Today, I am compelled to catalyze a paradigm shift. My fervent wish is to resonate with the world, urging our current generation and those that follow to reconsider how they approach circumstances and the environments they expose their children to. It's time to discard the notion that our children are oblivious or that certain matters can be swept under the rug, leaving them uninformed. Let's collectively adopt a new mindset — one that fosters open communication and rejects the outdated belief that what happens within the confines of our homes should stay confined.

I need the world to know that I was only four years old when my mom was murdered, and I can recall vivid events prior to her death in 1982. I distinctly remember my mom leaving my brother and me home at night while she went across the street to the club called the Post. It stood proudly on the West side of Las Vegas, Nevada, at the corner of H and Doolittle, nestled in the heart of our undeveloped neighborhood. One night, my mom left us alone, and in the absence of supervision, we indulged in childlike antics, overturning furniture in playful exploration. When she returned, we hurriedly restored everything to its rightful place.

Another memory etched in my mind involves a visit from a man on a motorcycle to our apartment. I recall the joyous interaction between my mom, my brother, myself, and this individual. Laughter filled the room as we engaged in playful camaraderie. However, as the man requested a private conversation with our mother, they retreated to the back bedroom, closing the door behind them. When he left abruptly, our mother emerged, not walking, but crawling on the floor. The inexplicable sight left me questioning the events behind that closed door. What transpired during that private conversation? The mystery endures, and to this day, I remain uncertain. What I do comprehend now is that during those formative years, both positive and negative seeds were being sown, influencing my early development.

After a brief interval, a knock echoed through the front door, and to our relief, it was our cousin, Alema. It seemed she had dropped by to assist our mom with the responsibilities concerning my brother and me. The only clear memory I have is of Alema helping us retrieve food from the refrigerator. Her presence was a welcome relief because, at that moment, our mother was in no condition to manage those tasks. Unfortunately, the nature of the challenges my mother was grappling with remains unknown to me to this very day. She maintained a steadfast silence, and our cousin, Alema, also refrained from sharing any details. If they did discuss the issues, it certainly wasn't in our presence.

Another memory involving Moon Dog at our apartment haunts my recollection. In the dead of night, we were fast asleep when the shattering sound of glass disrupted our peace — our bathroom window had been broken. In a tense moment, I recall my mom reaching for Moon Dog's gun, only for him to swiftly take it from her. We hastily dressed and left in his car. As we drove away, I spotted my dad and his twin brother standing by the side of the building. Overwhelmed with the desire to be with my dad, I started crying, but my mom insisted we continue to Moon Dog's house instead.

Back then, my mom had my brother and me share the bed with her and Moon Dog. In retrospect, I've come to understand that having kids sleep in the same bed with a parent and their partner may not always be a prudent choice. If one chooses to do so, it becomes crucial to shield the children from exposure to adult content. While many of us may have engaged in this practice, it's essential to recognize that such situations can mark the initial exposure to adult content for children. Though we might all be guilty of this oversight, it's important to consider the impacts on the children and the importance of modeling the purity we wish to instill.

As parents, we often find ourselves perplexed when witnessing our children displaying behaviors that leave us questioning their origins. It's crucial for us to be brutally honest with ourselves, acknowledging that we inadvertently expose our children to various influences when we aren't vigilant. The alarming reality is that children worldwide are getting entangled in gangs, and our initial instinct is to point fingers at those directly involved. However, a more honest reflection reveals that the primary responsibility lies with us as parents. We are failing to guide our children away from wrongdoing, and in some cases, we are the ones introducing them to a world tainted by corruption.

Positive role models within our homes are becoming increasingly scarce. Some fathers even lead these gangs, emulating styles that adversely influence young men. Mothers, too, find themselves ensnared in cycles of prostitution, perpetuating a damaging pattern in our communities. Men, having made a series of poor decisions, now face job market rejection, yet instead of imparting crucial life lessons to their sons, they inadvertently showcase negative examples. Consequently, these children grow up mirroring the destructive behaviors of their parents, perpetuating a cycle of prostitution, drug dealing, and addiction simply to survive within that lifestyle. The need for honest self-reflection and proactive parental guidance becomes increasingly evident to break this detrimental cycle.

I remember an incident where my mom leaped out of someone's car, resulting in a head injury. The reason behind her impulsive action remained unknown to me. It appears my mom was constantly entangled in troublesome situations, as if adversity trailed her wherever she went. With the perspective of age, I can now discern the recurring patterns in my mom's life. However, during my youth, I absorbed a particular way of life without discerning its moral implications. Right or wrong, it was a lifestyle ingrained in me from a very young age.

As I reflect on my mother's actions, especially the episode where she hastily exited a car, sustaining a head injury, the reasons behind such incidents eluded me in my younger years. It appears trouble had a way of finding her, persistently following her footsteps. Now, with the benefit of age, I recognize the cyclical nature of my mom's life. During my formative years, I was imbibing a way of life, devoid of a clear moral compass. It wasn't about distinguishing right from wrong; it was merely a way of life, deeply embedded in me from an early age.

CHAPTER FOUR
ECHOES OF SILENCE

In the aftermath of losing our mother, my brother and I outwardly appeared to acclimate swiftly to our new surroundings. Yet, beneath the surface, we grappled with an unspoken sense of profound loss. Occasional visits from our father, who would drop by our grandmother's house with money in hand after getting paid, remain vivid in my recollections. Reflecting on those times, it baffles me how much trust I invested in people, even during those early years.

I can vividly recall my dad during those visits, exuding happiness and excitement as he handed us cash. While my brother eagerly pocketed his share and left, I, trusting my grandmother with my portion, would later request it back when my dad returned to collect it.

As this routine persisted, my grandmother grew increasingly frustrated with my dad's habit of giving me money only to retrieve it later. Despite her objections, I persistently pleaded with her to hand it over, convinced he would honor his promise—though he never did. The disappointment deepened when, after refusing to surrender the money, my dad ceased his visits. This was particularly devastating as I had always treasured those moments, however brief. Looking back, I now realize that this pattern of accepting less in my relationships was rooted in the unmet need for acceptance from my father, leading me to settle. Reflecting on those times, I also recall the hurtful words he uttered when my brother resisted giving up his share. In a surprising revelation, after all those years, my dad declared he was not the father of my brother. It was a stark reminder that people often exhibit kindness only when it benefits them, a truth I reluctantly played along with.

Growing up, my dad was rarely present for my brother and me, entangled in his struggles with drugs and alcohol. The weight of our mom's death seemed to compound his challenges, making any attempt to discuss her a conversation he actively avoided. Despite his minimal involvement during my formative years, I clung to the notion of being a daddy's girl, yearning for the love of a father who seemed elusive. Hope persisted within me that one day he would overcome his battles, and my prayers were consistently directed to that end. Despite the difficulties he faced, I would have sacrificed anything just to spend time with him.

His visits brought unparalleled joy, transforming me into the happiest girl in the world. However, bidding him farewell became a heartbreaking struggle for me. I would cry and plead for him to take me with him, chasing after him in desperation. This emotional display stirred frustration within my family, particularly my aunt, who had to chase after me. At that time, it felt as though they couldn't grasp the depth of my longing, leaving me feeling empty and bewildered.

Despite my dad grappling with his own challenges, my grandmother occasionally allowed us to spend days with him during visits. Whether it was due to his sister's plea or some other intervention, I felt genuinely grateful. These visits typically took place at our aunt's house, offering us the chance to connect with her and our other cousins. However, the environment there starkly contrasted with our grandmother's home. It was often messy, with clothes strewn about, and dirty dishes scattered throughout. Unlike our grandmother, who maintained a disciplined and structured household, this setting was carefree, where chores and cleaning were not a priority.

Yet, the joy of spending time with our dad overshadowed the less-than-ideal surroundings. The location or the conditions didn't matter; we were simply elated to have that time together. While our grandmother instilled discipline and structure, the atmosphere at our aunt's was characterized by a more relaxed approach, allowing for freedom and a sense of enjoyment.

Frequently, my grandmother facilitated active involvement from my dad's side of the family, particularly Aunt Velma, who conveniently lived right next door. On one memorable occasion, my brother and I were granted permission to visit Aunt Velma's granddaughter's house, becoming the hub for various constructive activities. This included swimming and engaging in performing arts, where a choreographer taught me the art of dance. Learning a dance routine was immensely enjoyable, and the highlight was performing it at the Huntridge Theater in Las Vegas.

Reflecting on these experiences, I wished for more accessible activities tailored for families like ours, with limited financial resources. It would have been wonderful to have a broader range of low-cost opportunities that catered to individuals who, like us, couldn't afford to participate in such enriching experiences.

Empowering our children with effective communication skills is paramount. These are the moments when we guide them in finding their voice, demonstrating how to express their needs positively. Teaching them to recognize when their boundaries are violated is crucial, fostering an environment where speaking up is not only encouraged but seen as necessary. Unspoken issues often linger beneath the surface, and unless we actively inquire, they may never emerge until the damage is irreversible. This cycle perpetuates when unaddressed pain leads individuals to inflict harm on others, underscoring the critical importance of open dialogue and the proactive teaching of communication skills.

Despite the positive experiences, I also encountered some profoundly negative ones, often experiencing violations. Regrettably, I chose to remain silent, oblivious to the lasting impact it would have on me and the subsequent influence on my actions and worldview. This silence also instilled a deep-seated fear within me, particularly the fear of speaking up.

Little did I comprehend at that moment that my silence would set in motion a relentless cycle of concealed abuse, diminished self-esteem, substance misuse, interpersonal challenges, and mental health struggles.

Chapter Five
Unveiling Shadows

In the intricate tapestry of caring for young children, an essential duty lies in safeguarding not only their physical well-being but also their interactions with those in their immediate environment. Entrusting our children to various caregivers may inadvertently expose them to potential risks, as those we perceive as safe may not always be. The urgency in emphasizing this caution stems from my own encounters with cycles of molestation that originated not from strangers, but from individuals seemingly close to our family, hidden in plain sight.

One vivid memory involves an elderly woman residing next door to my maternal grandmother's house. She operated a small shop selling candy, soda, pickles, and treats for the neighborhood kids. Her older children, significantly older than my brother and me, occasionally interacted with us. Despite the age gap, one of them entered my grandmother's backyard one day, not to join our play but merely to linger. Uncomfortable with his presence, I wanted him to leave, but my grandmother, upon discovering us, scolded me harshly and ordered me inside. Her stern tone heightened my fear, leaving me feeling in the wrong. In that moment, I wished for a different response—one that involved sitting down, asking questions, and helping me find my voice.

Unfortunately, the situation unfolded differently, leaving words unspoken and my voice silenced once again.

Given that my grandmother likely overheard us in the backyard, it's crucial to empathize with children in such situations. Responding with harshness may not always be warranted, especially when a complete understanding of the circumstances is lacking. Although I chose not to disclose the incident, sensing my grandmother's reluctance to acknowledge it, I never returned to the backyard with that person. Despite his proximity and occasional attempts to beckon me over, I consistently avoided him throughout my elementary school years. My connection with God, nurtured in the church, provided solace, as I believed that nothing remained hidden from God's sight.

In hindsight, I recall people invoking the biblical passage "you shall reap what you sow." Looking back, I realize I was shielded from a potential predator. One day, while playing in my grandmother's driveway, I witnessed him collapsing to the ground in the driveway next to ours. Despite efforts and an ambulance being called, they couldn't arrive in time, and his life ended abruptly before my eyes. As I looked at him, thoughts of the harm he had done flashed through my mind, and I felt a profound sense of gratitude that God had protected me. This incident marked my initial connection to the belief that God watches over His children.

Another occasion etched in my memory involves the police questioning my grandmother about an incident involving someone close to me. In a room with my grandmother and aunt, I admitted knowledge of the situation. In response, my grandmother, with sternness and a high-pitched voice, demanded to know why I hadn't spoken up earlier. Fear etched on my face, I felt in trouble again. My aunt, pleading on my behalf, explained that I hesitated because I often felt disbelieved. I remained silent because, fundamentally, I believed the truth was frequently dismissed. This experience raised a pivotal question: How can a child develop an authentic voice when met with constant reprimand? Life's challenges are meant to be navigated with the support of those around you.

The individual close to me had my support, advocating for her before law enforcement arrived. Unfortunately, her grandmother doubted her and sided with the other party. It's a disheartening reality, underscoring the reluctance to conduct thorough investigations into claims people make. In our pursuit of personal desires, we sometimes jeopardize the safety of those under our care. Acknowledging the truth about someone we deeply love can be challenging, and we've all likely experienced this vulnerability. True change becomes elusive if one refuses to confront the reality. Embracing the truth is paramount, as it liberates us from the shackles of falsehood. The analogy of Jesus' sacrifice emphasizes the importance of confessing our sins for freedom from shame. Transformation and walking in the newness of Christ require acknowledging and addressing our own struggles.

I never had the chance to see my friend again as she was relocated from her grandparents' house for her own well-being. She had fallen prey to a predator whose actions persisted even after her removal, as his wife defended him. The details of the officers' actions or the aftermath of their investigation remain uncertain, but the crucial outcome was her removal from that harmful situation, for which I am grateful. Personally, I managed to avoid becoming a victim by keeping my distance. Even when I vehemently demanded to be released from his house, it didn't deter him from his disturbing pursuits. The specifics of his fate escape my memory, but as we all traverse this transient existence, we will eventually transcend our mortal forms. Advocating for one another and standing up for what is right remains of utmost importance.

CHAPTER SIX
VEILED INDEPENDENCE

At the tender age of twelve, I found myself gravitating toward the company of older girls, much to my grandmother's dismay. She perceived them as negative influences and aimed to distance me from their circle. One Saturday morning, when a friend came by, seeking companionship, I sought permission from my grandmother. However, her denial fueled frustration, leading me to accuse her of attempting to isolate me from my friends. In a sudden and unexpected moment, her hand struck my face, leaving my nose bleeding. Taken aback, she swiftly attended to me, cautioning me to mind my words.

In the aftermath of that incident, I chose silence over confrontation. I diligently carried out household tasks without protest, avoiding another harsh response. Instead of openly expressing my emotions, I embraced a new strategy—sneakiness. Incapable of communicating openly, I chose to act covertly. While complying with chores, I would slip out of the back door unnoticed by my grandmother. Socializing with friends offered a sense of liberation; no one dictated our actions, and we could freely share our thoughts without judgment.

What commenced as a few hours of socializing gradually transformed into an all-day, overnight routine. Despite facing repercussions for staying out all night, the allure of independence beckoned me repeatedly. Defiant and feeling that no one had the right to control me, I pursued my desires, reasoning that lacking a mother meant no one could dictate my choices.

Venturing out late at night at such a young age presented significant risks. Young girls in this scenario are exposed to a world fraught with violence and crime, rendering them vulnerable to predatory individuals seeking to exploit them. The old adage, "the freaks come out at night," rings true, underscoring the potential dangers. Nighttime becomes synonymous with a lifestyle involving partying, drugs, alcohol, illicit encounters, and criminal activities. Men with questionable intentions actively seek opportunities during these hours, and many women find themselves entangled in this perilous lifestyle while running away from home, violating curfew laws, or rebelling against parental guidance. This prompts the question of why any respectable woman would choose to roam the streets during the late hours of the night.

The older girls I associated with had a penchant for hopping into men's cars for joy rides or party ventures. This made me profoundly uncomfortable, prompting me to devise a strategy where the older girls would take the car while they went into stores to purchase alcohol. Given my young age and the fact that I was already underage, I was not eager to uncover where these excursions might lead. I reasoned that taking the car seemed a safer option than potentially ending up in a hotel or motel room with them, engaging in activities I preferred not to imagine. The uncertainty of our return made such scenarios out of the question for me, and I would find any excuse to extricate myself from these situations.

Spending time with these older girls during the late hours exposed me to perilous situations, including gang initiations involving criminal activities such as fast-food robberies, bystander shootings, and fist-fighting initiations—none of which I desired any part of. Despite the pressures of street culture, I clung to my fear of the Lord, grounded in a robust upbringing in Christ Jesus that had instilled virtuous values in me. However, the street code dictated severe consequences for those who divulged information, and witnessing a crime meant turning a blind eye. This mindset poses a serious threat to our society and families, as it adversely affects our homes.

In the silent shadows of my childhood, I harbored a secret woven into the fabric of the violence that pervaded my daily existence. Growing up amidst an atmosphere tainted by brutality demanded a cloak of discretion—a survival tactic to navigate hazardous waters. In the crucible of such an environment, the seeds of adaptation and indifference toward others' opinions took root within me. Witnessing firsthand the ruthlessness inflicted by those harboring disdain, I observed a landscape marred by bullying and drive-by shootings, mere footsteps away from my grandmother's dwelling. These were not distant strangers but the very individuals with whom we engaged in routine interactions. Silence became my refuge, a shield against the peril that lurked, for to utter a word could seamlessly render me a victim to the same malevolence. It was here that the tendrils of my profound fear found fertile ground to entwine and take hold.

CHAPTER SEVEN

A TUMULTUOUS ADOLESCENCE

My teenage years unraveled into a complex web of challenges, a consequence of my association with a circle steeped in negative influences. These early years were a haze of weed smoke, house parties, and the desperate act of running away from home. One night stands out vividly in my memory—a night that evolved into a nightmare after reveling with so-called friends.

The promise of a ride home came from one of the girls in the group, assuring me that an older gentleman, a heavyset African American adorned with a cross, would be my escort. Trusting her words, I entered his van, a decision that quickly turned harrowing. As we navigated the darkened streets, he ignored my directions home, revealing chilling intentions of a motel, payment, and an unspeakable demand. Overwhelmed and uncertain, I reluctantly agreed, but survival instincts kicked in.

Seizing a fleeting opportunity, I suggested a stop at a nearby 7 Eleven for refreshments. In that moment behind the store, he relinquished the keys, and as he disappeared into the store, I seized the moment. Jumping into the driver's seat, I sped away, leaving behind the ominous threat of a perilous encounter. Fear lingered, but relief washed over me as I escaped the clutches of that enigmatic man, spared from the unspeakable fate that loomed in the shadows.

Approaching the pivotal intersection of Lake Mead and H Street, panic surged within me once more. Fearing my grandmother's disapproval, I parked discreetly behind the church near H Street and Alexander junction. Opting for a silent journey, I covered the remaining distance to my house on foot. That night, shrouded in silence, I refrained from sharing my harrowing experience, quietly tending to myself before slipping into slumber.

The next day, checking on the van, I found it still in its clandestine spot. Rather than confide in a responsible adult, my friends and I impulsively chose to reclaim the van and embark on a joyride through Las Vegas. Naively dismissing any reservations, I justified our actions based on the man's wrongdoing.

About a week later, the van broke down on Martin Luther King near Bonanza, and we had to pull over. A police officer noticed our predicament and offered assistance, but the situation escalated when additional officers arrived with guns drawn. Compliance was our only recourse, and in the chaos, I realized the gravity of my actions. Admitting to taking the van to escape a perilous situation, I was informed that I would be arrested for auto theft, emphasizing that reporting the incident would have been the proper course.

Guilt and disbelief settled upon me. Despite my internal turmoil, a friend stepped forward, admitting to influencing my decision. Both of us faced the consequences of auto theft, with the officer releasing the others involved while we bore the brunt of the legal repercussions.

Sentenced to Caliente Youth Camp for nearly six months, I found myself at a pivotal juncture. My grandmother, troubled by my frequent escapades, played a crucial role in redirecting my path. In Caliente, I acquired communication skills and gained insights into the motivations behind my actions. Engaging in discussion groups provided a platform to explore instances when we veered off course and dissect the underlying reasons for our behavior.

This period marked a crucial juncture where I learned to delve into the intricacies of my emotions and cultivate awareness of my feelings. Negative actions often stemmed from emotions such as embarrassment, anger, guilt, isolation, or a desire to prove oneself. The power of articulating thoughts and feelings became clear, transforming my perspective.

During my brief stay at Caliente, I engaged in sports, attended school, and participated in meaningful activities. The environment shifted from resembling an institution for troubled youth to one focused on positive influences, adding excitement and imparting crucial lessons on constructive and positive environments.

Upon my return home, a distressing incident prompted me to seek refuge with my aunt after enduring a severe beating inflicted by my grandmother's husband. Unjustly targeted for something I had not done, I faced brutality with no witnesses, leaving me feeling defenseless. My aunt's intervention brought the truth to light, revealing that our cousin, not me, was responsible for the transgression.

Following these traumatic incidents, I descended into increasingly reckless behavior. Heavier drug use, entanglement with toxic men, and crossing paths with the father of my children became part of my reality. The gravity of the situation led me to the decision to leave home, vowing never to return.

CHAPTER EIGHT
A TURBULENT JOURNEY

Amidst the bustling city of Las Vegas, Miss Vegas found herself in a new chapter of her life, residing with her aunt on the East side. Enrolled at Eldorado High School, she had the opportunity to leapfrog the 8th grade, offering a fresh start after facing setbacks in her earlier academic years.

Her aunt's abode radiated beauty and comfort, reflecting her vibrant personality. Welcomed graciously into their family alongside two sons, Miss Vegas encountered counseling for the first time. Despite the picturesque beginning, fragments of loneliness and a sense of unequal treatment surfaced, stemming from the void left by her mother and the absence of her father.

Struggling to articulate these emotions, Miss Vegas yearned for familial warmth but found herself in a profound internal struggle. Seeking solace in misguided places, she unintentionally embraced negativity, overlooking the love that surrounded her.

Enrolled in counseling to heal deep-seated wounds, Miss Vegas's experience took an unexpected turn. The counselor failed to understand her struggles, leading to confusion and emotional vulnerability. Unable to express her turmoil, Miss Vegas sought comfort in a group of negative individuals, offering a distorted sense of belonging.

Despite her aunt's support, the growing distance between them was palpable. Miss Vegas's newfound companions became a substitute for the familial warmth she craved, intensifying her internal anxiety.

The repercussions of her counseling experience and internal turmoil led to discord in her aunt's household. Miss Vegas found herself placed in a group home, resulting in a transfer to Clark High School, surrounded by troubled youths.

In a twist of fate, Miss Vegas formed a nighttime alliance with an older roommate, leading to a harrowing incident at her roommate's boyfriend's house. Refusing advances, Miss Vegas faced a violent attack outside the apartment complex, betrayed by onlookers who remained indifferent.

Shattered and unable to recall subsequent events, Miss Vegas somehow ended up back in her grandmother's care during the period of healing. A fateful encounter near Lake Mead and D Street introduced her to the man who would become the father of her children, marking another unexpected turn in her tumultuous journey.

CHAPTER NINE

TANGLED IN THE WEB

The introduction to the man who would become the father of my children marked a significant turning point, but little did I know the complexities that lay ahead. He, eleven years my senior, pursued me with an intensity that both intrigued and alarmed me. Initially, fear lingered, and I insisted on bringing a friend along when meeting him, seeking safety in numbers until comfort settled in.

As we got to know each other, the allure of his world became magnetic, drawing me in like a moth to a flame. I found solace in his company, and slowly, my visits to his place transformed into a means of escape from the tumultuous environment I called home.

However, the shadows lurking beneath the surface began to reveal themselves. His possessiveness escalated, turning into a consuming jealousy that cast a dark shadow over our relationship. Even innocent interactions, like sitting at the table to watch his sisters and their boyfriends play card games, triggered his irrational rage.

One particular incident etched itself into my memory. Amidst the card games, he summoned me away from the table into the bedroom. I sat on the dresser with a mirror behind me, unsuspecting of the storm that was about to unfold. Without warning, he pushed my head into the glass, a cruel and bewildering act that left me shocked and in tears. His words were sharp, commanding me to stay out of "these guys' faces." Confused, scared, and hurt, I grappled with the aftermath of this sudden burst of violence.

In the twisted dance of our relationship, apologies became a familiar soundtrack. He would sweet-talk me, buy gifts, and assure me that it wouldn't happen again. The cycle of mistreatment followed by remorse created a psychological trap, and I found myself unable to break free.

He assumed the role of provider, catering to my needs as I was too young to work. In my naivety, I mistook his actions for love. The more he apologized, the more guilt I felt about leaving, convinced that he could change. His manipulation tightened its grip on me, and I became entangled in the web of abuse, unable to discern between love and control.

As time passed, the abuse escalated. Small gestures of kindness were overshadowed by explosive reactions to the smallest perceived slights. If someone asked me for a cigarette, and I offered it, he would erupt in anger, turning a simple act of kindness into a battleground. The more I tried to accommodate, the more volatile the situation became.

Infidelity became a dark undercurrent in our relationship. Caught in the throes of his unfaithfulness, he would vehemently deny any wrongdoing, spinning webs of lies that left me questioning my own sanity. Each revelation plunged me deeper into a world of physical altercations, as the women involved confronted me, forcing me to defend myself against their aggression.

His sister, a silent spectator to the chaos, would not intervene but rather encouraged the conflicts, transforming them into a sick form of entertainment. They would sit around, laughing, and relishing the violence, as if my pain were a source of amusement.

The more ensnared I became, the more he reveled in the power he held over me. Obsession fueled his actions, leaving me exposed and vulnerable to physical harm. The once enticing escape had become a trap, and I found myself trapped in a toxic cycle that seemed impossible to break.

CHAPTER TEN
TANGLED IN SHADOWS

In the shadowy web of my tumultuous relationship, I grappled with the illusion of love woven into the fabric of extreme jealousy. As he oscillated between abuse and false expressions of affection, I found myself entangled in a twisted dance, where each step seemed to draw me deeper into a dark abyss.

His pretense of reluctance to let me go masked the true nature of our connection—a toxic bond fueled by manipulation and control. The echoes of his possessiveness reverberated through our lives, and in a bid for survival, he introduced me to the gritty streets of Downtown Las Vegas, where selling drugs became our means of existence.

In the labyrinth of my emotions, I resisted the idea of having children, a notion he persistently pushed. The more I vocalized my aversion to motherhood, the tighter he clamped down on the concept, steering me away from the thought of building a family. The weight of my petite frame was emphasized by the provocative clothes he bought for me, attracting unwanted attention, and perpetuating my vulnerability.

His dominance extended beyond the streets; it infiltrated my very sense of self. I became a timid soul, avoiding eye contact and lowering my gaze in fear of his unpredictable wrath.

Approaching others with my head down, I navigated the world with trepidation, afraid that any interaction might provoke his anger, leading to yet another violent encounter.

In the midst of this chaos, a glimmer of intervention emerged. My aunt, spotting me downtown, would follow in her car, attempting to rescue me from the clutches of this destructive relationship. She knew the danger I was in, working tirelessly to pull me away from the only person I had convinced myself loved me.

Her persistence reached a breaking point one day when she successfully trailed me to my destination. Recognizing the imminent threat, she called the police in a desperate bid to intervene. The consequences were swift and unforgiving, as the handcuffs tightened around my wrists once again, marking my second entry into the confines of Caliente Youth Camp.

Sentenced to five months, the bars of the detention center became both a physical and metaphorical representation of the entrapment I felt in my life. The world outside had become a distant memory, and as the days turned into months, I grappled with the reality of my choices and the chains that bound me. The fleeting illusion of love had led me into a labyrinth of darkness, and as the doors closed behind me, I confronted the harsh truth that liberation seemed elusive in the shadows of my own making.

Chapter Eleven
Shadows of Escape

As the van rumbled along the road, I felt the weight of my impending fate settle over me. The air inside the vehicle hung heavy with a mix of uncertainty and resignation. I knew the path that lay ahead—a journey to Caliente Youth Camp awaited me, a place I had once escaped only to find myself returning.

In a desperate attempt to elude the inevitable, I seized an opportunity on Civic Center Drive. The van slowed, and as the door creaked open, I leaped out, my heart pounding with a fierce determination to break free from the chains that bound me. The cold pavement met my feet as I sprinted, the rhythmic thud of my steps echoing a desperate plea for liberation.

The correction officer, fueled by frustration and determination, pursued me with unwavering resolve. Panic fueled my flight, my breaths quickening with each stride. I darted behind buildings, weaving through the labyrinth of streets, hoping to outsmart the relentless chase that followed.

In a moment of respite, I found refuge behind a garbage can in an apartment building. The shadows concealed me, but the officer's persistence prevailed. He discovered my hiding place, and the fleeting taste of freedom dissolved into the harsh reality of capture.

Upon reaching Caliente Youth Camp, the consequences of my escape attempt were swift and severe. The correction officer, visibly upset by the ordeal, stripped down a room and designated it as my confined space. Branded a "flight risk," I was adorned with thong shoes, a visual marker of my perceived threat to the order of the camp.

I resisted the confines of the room, the walls closing in on me as my cries pierced the air. Unmoved by my distress, the correction officer, burdened by the chase I had led him through, sought to silence me. In an act devoid of mercy, he took a small hand-held metal bar and pressed it relentlessly against the front bone of my leg.

The pain shot through me, intensifying with each scream that escaped my lips. I threatened to expose his brutality, but his response was a chilling assurance that nobody would believe me. The power dynamics were skewed, and within the constraints of monitored calls, there were things left unspoken, lest the phones be abruptly disconnected.

I bore the weight of my silence, the unspoken trauma etched into my flesh and imprinted on my spirit. The chase down Civic Center Drive became a haunting memory, a reminder of the lengths I had gone to escape a fate that seemed inescapable. As the days unfolded within the confines of Caliente, I navigated a world where cries for help were met with cold indifference, and the shadows of escape only led to darker corridors of pain.

The walls of the empty cell in Caliente, once a confining testament to my perceived threat, began to release their hold on me. Through a display of good behavior and a commitment to the program, I managed to shed the "flight risk" label that had marked me. The correction officer's iron grip on my existence slowly loosened, allowing me to reintegrate into the fabric of Caliente Youth Camp.

As I transitioned from solitary confinement to participation with the other cottage girls, I felt a mix of relief and trepidation. My familiarity with the program, having returned for a second time, allowed me to navigate the group discussions with a sense of ease. Yet, beneath the surface, I grappled with the lingering shadows of anger that had taken residence within me.

Engaging in group discussions, attending sports, and diligently pursuing my studies became my lifelines within the structured environment of Caliente. The routine, though challenging, provided a framework for self-reflection and growth. With each passing day, I worked through the layers of anger that had accumulated within me, seeking solace and understanding within the supportive community of my fellow residents.

Within the span of five months, my journey through Caliente Youth Camp reached a pivotal moment. The program, designed to rehabilitate troubled youth, had become a crucible of transformation for me. The recognition of my efforts and commitment to change granted me the release to go home. The once-daunting walls of confinement now stood behind me, as I stepped into the uncertain terrain of freedom, carrying with me the lessons learned and the resilience forged in the crucible of Caliente.

Chapter Twelve
A New Beginning

The transition from the structured confines of Caliente to the warm embrace of my aunt's home in Lancaster, California, marked a profound shift in my life's trajectory. My aunt and uncle, both active-duty members of the Air Force, opened their doors to provide me with a fresh start and a chance to experience life in a different environment.

The prospect of a new beginning filled me with a sense of hope and excitement. My aunt's intention was clear – to expose me to a kinder, more nurturing environment that would offer me opportunities beyond the challenges that had defined my past. As I embarked on this journey, I carried with me the lessons learned and the determination to reshape my future.

Arriving at their home, I was greeted not only with open arms but with the genuine desire to provide me with everything I needed. My aunt, a pillar of strength and kindness, became a beacon of stability in my life. The bustling air of Lancaster was a far cry from the tumultuous streets of Las Vegas, offering a stark contrast that allowed me to breathe freely.

Enrolled in a school situated just outside the military base, I found myself immersed in a supportive academic environment. To bolster my education, my uncle took on the role of a dedicated tutor, guiding me through the intricacies of my studies. The impact was palpable, and my academic performance soared, reflecting the newfound stability and encouragement surrounding me.

But beyond the academic realm, it was the emotional support that became the cornerstone of my healing. My aunt's love was a balm for my wounded spirit. When sadness or despair threatened to creep in, she would enter the room, offering comfort with a simple gesture or a reassuring presence. In those moments, I felt the warmth of a genuine family, a feeling that had eluded me for so long.

No longer did I feel adrift or abandoned. My aunt made a conscious effort to be there for me, to sit with me in times of brokenness, and to extend a hand of compassion when I needed it most. This newfound sense of belonging was transformative, and for the first time, I began to envision a future defined by love, support, and the promise of better days ahead.

CHAPTER THIRTEEN
A FATEFUL DETOUR

Despite the newfound stability and support in Lancaster, a single decision threatened to unravel the progress I had made. Sent back to Las Vegas for a routine doctor's visit, I found myself at a crossroads that would alter the course of my life. A chance encounter with the mother of my soon-to-be children's father led to an impromptu visit, and before I knew it, I had neglected to board the return flight to California.

Choosing to stay in Las Vegas opened the door to a series of events that would test the resilience of my newfound foundation. Spending time with him, the girl he was involved with, and his children's mother seemed harmless at first. One night, however, the undercurrents of alcohol and poor choices collided, culminating in a car crash that left us all injured.

As the car wrapped around a pole, chaos ensued, and I found myself in a disorienting blur. Head bleeding, vision impaired, I stumbled along Valley View towards Alta Drive. The ambulance eventually found me, taking me to the hospital, while he faced legal consequences. My grandmother, asserting that I was a runaway, and my aunt, pleading for my return, played pivotal roles in ensuring I made it back to the sanctuary of their home in Lancaster.

Returning home was a relief, marking the first time I truly felt a sense of belonging and support. However, the toxic cycle resumed when I allowed him to persuade me to disclose my aunt's address. Foolishly, I joined him on a journey back to Nevada, despite the recent incident where he had endangered our lives.

Upon our return to Las Vegas, the cycle of abuse persisted, and he once again proposed the idea of having a child together. This time, I acquiesced, and soon I was pregnant with my firstborn son, whom I named Steven. The gravity of his remarks about keeping me pregnant failed to register, and I would eventually become the mother of four of his children.

The journey of hope amidst adversity unfolds. Despite the challenges, hope was not lost. Too often, my children's father would taunt me, proclaiming that he would keep me "barefoot and pregnant." Though I had not envisioned a life filled with numerous children, his words became my reality. Following Steven's birth in 1996, I found myself expecting again this time with a precious little girl in 1997 whom I named Special. Embracing the role of motherhood to two beautiful children, I began to comprehend the profound responsibility of nurturing another life.

The birth of my daughter marked a pivotal moment. Determined to pursue my dreams, I endeavored to return to school to train as a medical assistant. Yet, amidst my aspirations, my children's father unleashed a torrent of abuse, both physical and emotional. His relentless sabotage, culminating in bruises and fear, thwarted my attempts to attend classes. Despite the turmoil, I refused to relinquish my dreams.

Amidst the turmoil and the scars of betrayal, I found solace in my unwavering faith. Strengthened by my belief in God, I clung to hope. Sunday mornings became a sanctuary as I ushered my three children to church, a steadfast commitment born from a desire to shield them from the shadows of my past.

Then, a divine whisper pierced through the chaos, urging me to gaze upon my children. In that moment, clarity dawned – I refused to replicate the pattern of abandonment that plagued my own upbringing. The echo of my mother's absence reverberated within me, igniting a fierce determination to carve a different path for my children.

The cycle of abuse endured for years, testing my endurance and strength. It wasn't until the age of 21 that I found the courage to break free from the shackles of an abusive relationship. The decision to leave marked the beginning of a journey toward self-discovery and resilience, as I vowed never to return to a life marred by mistreatment and violence.

Chapter Fourteen
Breaking the Chains

The ominous prophecy from the father of my children echoed in my ears as he repeatedly claimed that when I turned 21, I would finally leave him. Years of fervent prayers and dreams filled with signs from God seemed to pave the way for the courage I needed to escape the year-long abusive relationship that had nearly consumed me.

After a night of intense partying and substance abuse, I woke up disoriented, my pants down, questioning what had transpired. When I confronted him, he denied any wrongdoing. But this time, unlike the countless instances before, I found a newfound strength and resolve within me.

The tipping point came after a concert, where we indulged heavily in substances. That night, as I lay unconscious, a resolve formed within me to leave. When I awoke, I gathered my belongings and, for the first time, walked away from the father of my three children. Guided by premonitions of infidelity that God had bestowed upon me, and fueled by the weight of accumulated abuse, I knew it was time to break free.

Shortly after my departure, I found myself pregnant with another boy, whom I later named Kyle. While I allowed occasional visits between him and the children, the encounters turned violent, prompting me to prioritize the safety and well-being of myself and my children.

Leaving him didn't sit well with him, and the threats began to escalate. Fear consumed me, leaving me forgetful and scared, especially when alone or in the dark. Nightmares became a reality when he showed up one evening, breaking my window and sending me into a state of shock. I locked myself in the bathroom, unable to remember how to call the police but instinctively calling my grandmother instead.

As she arrived, her frustration was evident. Unaware of the depth of my torture, she chided me for not defending myself better. The instinct to cut the lights and confront the intruder in the darkness was foreign to me—I was drowning in fear, and those around me struggled to comprehend the extent of my suffering.

In the aftermath of that night, I began the slow and painful process of healing, trying to piece together the fragments of my shattered self. The decision to leave marked the beginning of a journey towards self-preservation and recovery, as I sought to build a life free from the shadows of abuse and violence.

Amidst the shadows of my healing journey, a semblance of peace appeared when my brother confronted the father of my children, issuing a stern warning to stay away from me. For a while, it seemed like a reprieve, a moment of respite from the constant fear that had plagued me.

However, a tragic turn awaited me when his sister approached, requesting my company on a trip to California to pick up her son. In an unexpected twist, the father of my children insisted on joining the journey to collect his own son. A foreboding sense of unease settled over me as I reluctantly agreed to share the ride, unaware that this decision would lead to an ominous chapter in my life.

As we embarked on the trip, tension lingered in the air. The weight of the past and the fear of the unknown cast a pall over the journey. Little did I know that the echoes of our shared history would reverberate in the hours to come, ultimately leading to a tragic and life-altering event.

CHAPTER FIFTEEN

SHADOWS OF A BROKEN NIGHT

The journey to California, initially intended as a swift turnaround to collect the children, took an unforeseen dark turn. The father of my kids, his sister, and I set out on what would become a harrowing odyssey. As we reached California, the atmosphere grew tense, poisoned by the fumes of alcohol and escalating hostility.

His demeanor shifted, and the veneer of civility crumbled under the influence of alcohol. I tried to maintain a calm and reassuring tone, emphasizing that the children would remain an integral part of his life. Yet, my attempts at de-escalation proved futile as he descended into a verbal barrage, hurling insults and demeaning me. My spirit wearied under the weight of his cruel words, and internal nervousness crept in.

In the confines of his mother's house, the situation escalated beyond control. Cornered and defenseless, I found myself subjected to a violent assault. His fists rained down on my face, and I could do nothing but cry out, "Lord Jesus, help me!" The brutality continued as he stomped on me, leaving me battered on the floor. In a moment of divine intervention, he recoiled in shock, allowing me to break free and run.

Dazed and bloodied, I fled until I reached an abandoned gas station with payphones. I dialed 911, my voice trembling as I recounted the horror I had endured. The police arrived, providing a lifeline amidst the darkness. They drove me around in search of the assailant, encountering resistance and deceit from his family. His sister, who held the phone during the ordeal, remained complicit in their cover-up.

The officer guided me to the freeway, and I returned home to a sleeping brother who awoke to the ghastly sight of my battered face. Infuriated, he vowed to seek justice. His anger surged, leading him to confront the assailant at Seven Seas club, attempting to meet out a similar punishment. Chaos ensued, and my intervention prevented further bloodshed, but retribution still loomed.

In a twisted turn, I discovered the insidious reality of covert drug use. Unbeknownst to me, he had been placing cocaine in my nose while I slept, rendering me a zombie-like existence. A revelation from a girl he was involved with brought this dark secret to light. Disgusted and betrayed, I distanced myself from him, but the toxic allure of substance abuse crept into my life, a haunting echo of the torment I had endured.

Chapter Sixteen

A Journey to Redemption

Emerging from the shadows of a toxic relationship, I faced the daunting task of rebuilding my life, a journey marked by resilience and divine intervention. The embarrassment of bearing visible scars to work became a testament to the strength within, and I turned my gaze toward the light at the end of a long, arduous tunnel.

With determination as my compass, I embarked on a path to education, enrolling in school to expand my horizons and escape the clutches of a troubled past. The echoes of God's forgiveness reverberated in my soul, guiding me toward a brighter future. Destiny helpers, benevolent figures placed strategically in my path, emerged to aid me on this transformative journey.

Creating a haven for my children became a priority, and against the odds, I secured a home where we could rebuild our shattered lives. God's grace became evident as I navigated through financial constraints and the challenges of single parenthood. Even in the midst of scarcity, my unwavering faith acted as a beacon, illuminating the path ahead.

Yet, the world around me remained steeped in violence and negativity. To shield my children from the tumultuous influences, I made the difficult choice to isolate myself from the chaos. Nights were spent in tears, fervently pleading with God to guide me through the trials and tribulations that threatened to engulf me.

The struggle was multifaceted, encompassing not only financial limitations but also the recurring specter of substance abuse. Despite the challenges, I pressed forward, driven by the belief that a brighter future awaited on the other side of adversity. Destiny helpers continued to manifest, offering support and encouragement when I needed it most.

In the crucible of life's hardships, I discovered the strength to rise above my circumstances. Each step forward became a testament to the transformative power of resilience and faith. The journey to redemption was not without its hurdles, but with God's grace and the aid of destiny helpers, I found solace in the hope that a new chapter awaited—one filled with promise, healing, and the triumph of the human spirit.

In the aftermath of tumultuous years, I found myself seeking refuge in the arms of an unwavering presence—God. As I rekindled my relationship with the divine, I discovered a sanctuary where unconditional love and grace transcended the scars of my past. God, never one to give up on me, became my anchor in the storm of life.

Returning to the embrace of the church, I felt the warm currents of spiritual solace wash over me. The pews became a sanctuary, and the hymns echoed the melodies of redemption. In the sacred space of worship, I found a community that embraced me despite the stains of my history. It was a place where forgiveness flowed freely, mirroring the boundless grace of a loving God.

A profound transformation took root within me as I nurtured a robust prayer life. In the quiet moments of communion with God, I laid bare my hopes, fears, and aspirations. The divine became my confidant, the source of strength that sustained me through the trials of life. With each prayer, I relinquished control, recognizing that God's plan far surpassed the limitations of my understanding.

The journey was arduous, but the unwavering presence of God by my side infused me with a renewed sense of purpose. I learned to depend on Him for everything, recognizing His guidance as a constant beacon in the ever-changing currents of life. No longer did I face the challenges alone; I stood fortified by the divine love that surrounded me.

Through the power of prayer and a deepening relationship with God, I witnessed the gradual transformation of my life. The shadows of my past began to dissipate, replaced by the radiant light of hope and redemption. In moments of despair, God's love remained a steadfast companion, reminding me that His mercy was boundless and His forgiveness infinite.

As the pages of my life turned, the narrative shifted from one of turmoil to a testament of resilience and faith. God's unwavering presence and the solace found in His embrace became the foundation upon which I rebuilt my life. The journey of redemption continued, guided by the divine hand that never ceased to lead me toward a brighter tomorrow.

Closing and Takeaways

As you reach the end of "Secrets of a Child Left Behind: Hope Was Not Lost," take a moment to reflect on the profound journey you've just experienced. This narrative has taken you through the depths of despair, illuminated by the flickering ember of hope that refuses to be extinguished. It's a story of resilience, courage, and the indomitable spirit that can withstand even the harshest trials.

In the face of unimaginable adversity, the characters in this tale have not merely survived; they have overcome. The author's courage in unraveling the complexities of their journey is an invitation to witness the strength found in unexpected places, the endurance of the human spirit, and the redemptive power of hope.

As you close this chapter, remember that this story is not just about one individual's life; it's a tapestry of shared experiences that can resonate with anyone who has faced trials, sought hope in adversity, or embraced the transformative power of resilience. It is a testament to the enduring belief that, even in the darkest hours, the glimmer of hope can guide us back to the light.

Takeaways from "Secrets of a Child Left Behind: Hope Was Not Lost":

1. **Resilience in Adversity: ** The narrative showcases the remarkable resilience of the human spirit in the face of unimaginable challenges. It is a testament to the idea that

resilience goes beyond mere survival; it is about finding strength and growth through adversity.

2. **The Transformative Power of Hope: ** This story emphasizes that hope, even in its most fragile form, can be a powerful catalyst for transformation. It serves as a reminder that holding onto hope, no matter how tenuous, can lead to profound change.

3. **Connection and Understanding: ** Through the characters' experiences, the book fosters a sense of connection and understanding. It invites readers to empathize with the struggles of others, recognizing that shared humanity can bridge gaps and bring solace.

4. **Facing Darkness with Faith: ** The author's unwavering faith in the face of attempts to silence the narrative is a testament to the power of belief. It encourages us to face darkness with faith, trusting that even in the bleakest moments, there is a guiding light.

Prepare yourself for Part 2 of this compelling journey. The introduction hints at the haunting shadows and desolation that await, promising a continuation of a narrative that explores the depths of the human experience. As you turn the page to the next chapter, carry with you the lessons of resilience, the inspiration of hope, and the understanding that, even in the darkest corridors, the strength to endure resides within.

Printed in the United States
by Baker & Taylor Publisher Services